Hairdressing is Fun

By Jaala Ozies

Library For All Ltd.

Library For All is an Australian not for profit organisation with a mission to make knowledge accessible to all via an innovative digital library solution. Visit us at libraryforall.org

Hairdressing is Fun

First published 2023

Published by Library For All Ltd
Email: info@libraryforall.org
URL: libraryforall.org

Our Yarning logo design by Jason Lee, Bidjipidji Art

Original illustrations by Angharad Neal-Williams

Hairdressing is Fun
Ozies, Jaala
ISBN: 978-1-922991-07-2
SKU03390

Hairdressing is Fun

We respect and honour Aboriginal and Torres Strait Islander Elders past, present and future. We acknowledge the stories, traditions and living cultures of Aboriginal and Torres Strait Islander peoples on this land and commit to building a brighter future together.

Hairdressers can blow-dry your hair.

Hairdressers can braid your hair.

Hairdressers can colour your hair.

Hairdressers can cut your hair.

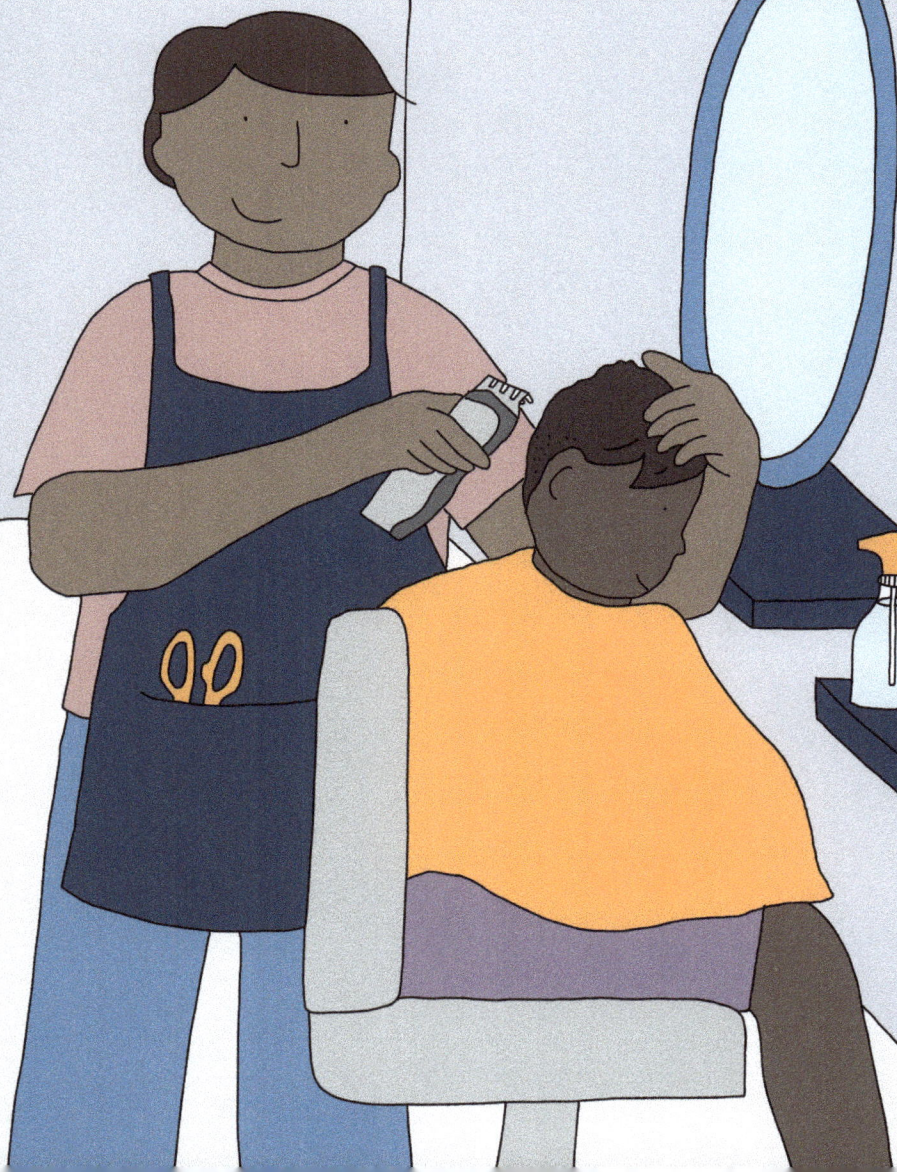

Hairdressers can
curl your hair.

Hairdressers can perm your hair.

Hairdressers can straighten your hair.

Hairdressers can
wash your hair.

Hairdressers can make you feel good about your hair.

You can use these questions to talk about this book with your family, friends and teachers.

What did you learn from this book?

Describe this book in one word. Funny? Scary? Colourful? Interesting?

How did this book make you feel when you finished reading it?

What was your favourite part of this book?

download our reader app
getlibraryforall.org

About the author

Jaala was born in Perth and now lives in Broome. She is from the Djugun, Karajarri, Nyikina, Kija and Gija Nations. Jaala loves going fishing and camping with her family. Her parents' stories were her favourite when she was a child.

Our Yarning

Want to discover more books from this collection? Our Yarning is a collection of books written by Aboriginal and Torres Strait Islander peoples across Australia.

We know that children learn better, and enjoy reading more, when they see themselves in the stories, characters and illustrations of the books they read.

To download the app, visit the Google Play Store on any Android device and search 'Our Yarning'.

libraryforall.org

www.ingramcontent.com/pod-product-compliance
Lightning Source LLC
Chambersburg PA
CBHW042346040426
42448CB00019B/3433